# THE LITTLE BLACK BOOK OF

# SUSHI

*The Essential Guide to the World of Sushi*

DAY ZSCHOCK

ILLUSTRATED BY KERREN BARBAS

PETER PAUPER PRESS, INC.
WHITE PLAINS, NEW YORK

TO MY FRIENDS AND FAMILY,
YOUNG AND OLD, WHO SHARE MY LOVE
OF LEARNING AND ADVENTURE

Designed by Heather Zschock

Illustrations copyright © 2005 Kerren Barbas

Copyright © 2005
Peter Pauper Press, Inc.
202 Mamaroneck Avenue
White Plains, NY 10601
All rights reserved
ISBN 1-59359-961-7
Printed in Hong Kong
7 6 5 4 3 2 1

Visit us at www.peterpauper.com

# THE LITTLE
# BLACK BOOK OF
# SUSHI

# CONTENTS

*irasshaimase!*
(welcome!)

O n a scale of 1 to 10, 1 being "Raw fish? No way!" and 10 being "I can't get enough of it," where are you on the sushi scale? No matter—whether you're a skeptic or a devotee, this *Little Black Book of Sushi* is sure to entertain and educate you about this exotic Japanese delicacy.

Japanese cuisine is not just about something to eat. It's about the careful selection and preparation of ingredients, and their elegant presentation. It's not just about taste, but also texture, color, and balance. It is food meant to delight the palate and to be "eaten" by the eyes. Sushi has it all.

Sushi is now available in grocery stores in most parts of the United States. Perhaps you've seen it being made and placed on small plastic trays, along with pouches of soy sauce and little mounds of green stuff. If that's your only experience with sushi, you really haven't begun to know what it's all about. It's a beginning step on the visual, culinary, and even spiritual journey toward fully experiencing sushi at its best.

Reading this book, you will discover the essence of sushi and how it evolved into what it is today. You'll learn about the ingredients and how they are carefully prepared and presented. You'll find a useful primer of the many types of sushi. You'll discover interesting facts about how to eat sushi and other ways to "mind your manners" at the table. Using the instructions and recipes, you can try your hand at becoming a sushi chef. Then, when you go to a sushi bar and see an *itamae-san* (master sushi chef) at work, you will appreciate his skill and be able to "talk the talk" with him.

Have fun, enjoy. *Itadakimasu* (Bon Appetit).

# sushi—past and present

Japan is an island chain strung out between the North Pacific Ocean and the Sea of Japan. It is a beautiful, mountainous country with little arable land, but its neighboring seas are abundant with an enormous variety of fish and shellfish. The unfriendly land has been terraced and cultivated for centuries by industrious, ingenious, and disciplined people. Rice, Japan's main crop, has been honored and acknowledged for more than a thousand years as a measure of a man's status in life. Rice and fish are Japan's treasures, and have been central to its culture for the past 1,500 years. These two foods have been key elements in the lives of the Japanese at every level of society. Sushi, as we know it today and as it evolved, has always been about these two "sacred" elements.

There are other aspects of the Japanese character and culture that are represented in

 the making, serving, and eating of sushi. The Japanese have a great respect for nature. Seasons regulate which foods are appropriate to be eaten; they must be as fresh and as close to their natural state as possible. This is evident in the minimalism of their aesthetics— whether it is in poetry, music, architecture, or cuisine—which feature balance, color, discipline, and simple elegance. Traditions and ceremonies are part of Japan's cultural life. If you have the opportunity to dine at a Japanese sushi bar you will experience all these qualities. Your food will be presented to you elegantly enhanced, not transformed. The staff will be gentle and hospitable, and you will enjoy a convivial yet peaceful dining experience. The sushi experience is an edible art form.

So exactly what is sushi? Is it raw fish? No, sushi, simply defined, is rice seasoned with sweet rice vinegar. More broadly, the current definition is sticky, vinegared rice with a topping or filling of fish, shellfish, egg, or vegetables. Raw fish is sashimi. It is sometimes confused with sushi and is the most popular ingredient in sushi. Without the rice it is not sushi. Sushi lovers often begin their meal with sashimi.

The Japanese made the first sushi, called *nare–zushi*, about 1,300 years ago. It was made by packing layers of cleaned, salted, raw fish between layers of rice. A heavy stone weight was placed on top and it was then left to ferment for as long as three years. As the rice fermented, it produced lactic acid that caused the fish to pickle and kept it from spoiling. Since the rice was sour, it was discarded and only the fish was consumed. In some parts of Japan a type of *nare-zushi*, first made about 1,200 years ago, is still produced. It is called

 *funa-zushi*, made with freshwater carp; the fish is eaten and the rice is thrown away. It has a very strong flavor and has little similarity to the modern sushi we know and love.

By 1600 the Japanese had developed *nama-nare*, (which means partially fermented). *Nama-nare* was matured for only a few days so the rice was only slightly sour and could be eaten. Thus, the custom of eating both the fish and the rice began. By 1650 Matsumoto Yoshiich, a doctor who lived in Edo (Tokyo was called Edo until 1868), started adding vinegar to the rice, which improved the taste of the rice and shortened the wait before the fish could be eaten. Perhaps out of habit, even cooked or marinated fish was still packed together with the rice for several days before being eaten.

In the early 1800s, small handfuls of sushi—vinegared rice, topped with cooked or marinated fish—began to be sold at small "take-out" stalls. In 1824 a chef named Hanaya Yohei from Edo began selling fresh, raw fish atop "fingers" of vinegared rice, and *nigiri-zushi* was born. Hanaya Yohei might well be considered the "father" of modern sushi.

## THE LEGENDARY HEALTH BENEFITS OF SUSHI

There is much to support the claims that sushi is a "health food." The Japanese, who have been eating sushi for hundreds of years, have about half the incidence of heart disease of Americans. This is probably because they eat far less saturated fat, and far more fish and fresh vegetables. Even the fattiest of raw fish contains fewer fat calories, by weight, than beef, pork, and even chicken. Breast cancer, which has been associated with having a diet high in fat, is rare in Japan.

The three main foods in the Japanese diet are fish, rice, and soy products. These three foods, along with vegetables and condiments, are the ingredients of sushi, perhaps the most popular food in Japan. The diet is a prescription for a long and healthy life.

Let's take a look at the health benefits of the common ingredients in sushi.

Fish

- Low in calories
- Low in fat
- Rich in protein
- A source of vitamin B12 and iodine
- Crab and oysters may lower cholesterol.
- Tuna and salmon are rich sources of omega-3 fatty acids, which are beneficial in preventing heart disease and stroke.

## Rice

- A source of protein and carbohydrates

## Vinegar

- Has antibacterial properties
- Aids digestion
- Is a natural skin conditioner

## Nori

- Rich in protein and minerals, especially iodine
- Rich in vitamins A, B1, C, and niacin

## Ginger and wasabi

- Have antibacterial properties
- Aid digestion
- Ginger alleviates nausea.
- Wasabi is rich in potassium, vitamin C.

## Fresh and pickled vegetables

- Rich in fiber, minerals, and vitamins

This all adds up to a very healthy diet. Sushi may be just what the doctor ordered!

A word should be said about the potential health risks of eating raw fish. The fish must be fresh or have been flash frozen at a very low temperature. It must be handled with care and cleanly stored. The Federal Food and Drug Administration (FDA) issues warnings against eating certain fish, especially raw fish. They test fish for the presence of parasites, the presence of PCBs, and for mercury levels. At the moment, there is an advisory that women of childbearing age and young children should not eat shark, swordfish, mackerel, or tilefish. In addition, it is advised that people with compromised immune systems should not eat raw fish.

# the basics

# THE RICE

Rice is so honored in Japan that the Emperor plants a small rice field each year within the imperial garden in Tokyo. He tends the garden himself as a ritual of respect for the role rice has played in the history and survival of his country.

Rice, the foundation of all Japanese food, was first grown in Japan as early as 200 BCE Rice production has always been a labor intensive, time-consuming, communal process. It was grown year after year in the same place, by generations of families, underpinning the structure and development of villages throughout Japanese history. Until the end of the 12th century, rice was mostly reserved for the aristocracy, but with the change to a feudal society rice became available to everyone. It was, and is today, eaten daily by the people of Japan. For this reason, if for no other, the ability to prepare perfect sushi rice, *sumeshi* (vinegared rice), is a chief measure of the skill of a sushi chef.

Good sushi rice must be prepared in a very particular way. Meticulous attention creates rice that is chewy-tender, moist, and clingy enough to be eaten with chopsticks or shaped into forms.

# The Fish

The variety and abundance of the fish in the sea around Japan is remarkable. Cold currents from the north meet with the Kuroshio, the warm plankton-rich Japan Current, spawning one of the world's finest fishing grounds. The proof: the Japanese are said to consume 3,000 different kinds of fish every day!

Tsukiji Fish Market in Tokyo is one of the largest and busiest fish markets in the world. Many years ago, the fish came mainly from Japanese waters; today 80 percent of the fish is frozen and comes from all over the world. Very early every morning the fresh and frozen fish arrive at the market. Each fish is tagged according to weight and place of origin, and otherwise prepared for inspection. A bell signals for bidding to begin. After the distributor completes his purchases, he arranges for the fish to be sent to other parts of the world, or he brings them to his own space in the market where he sells them to owners of fish shops, sushi shops, and restaurants. This process takes place in much the same way in similar markets all over the world.

Although it is usually assumed that most of the fish served at a sushi bar is fresh, this is not necessarily the case. Raw does not equal fresh. At least half of the sashimi served in the U.S. has been frozen to a temperature ranging from 10°F to -70°F. FDA regulations stipulate that fish sold to be eaten raw must be frozen first in order to kill parasites. (Tuna is the only fish exempt from this ruling.) This regulation is not always monitored, nor totally adhered to. There are benefits to freezing fish, however, despite the stigma against it. For example, fish that is out of season can be served at any time of the year. Frozen fish costs about half as

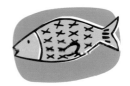

much as fresh, and this price difference can be extended to the diner. Perhaps most reassuring is the fact that even the most experienced chefs say they have a hard time telling the difference.

Moreover, eating particular types of fish raw can pose health risks. Salmon, for example, must be frozen if it is to be eaten raw because it may carry parasites. And freshwater fish should never be eaten raw because of the certain presence of parasites.

# THE TALE OF THE TUNA

For most of us, our first acquaintance with tuna was in the sandwiches Mom packed for school lunches, or the tuna casseroles made with cream of mushroom soup. In recent years, with the growing popularity of seared tuna, our taste for tuna has become more sophisticated. Tuna for sushi is another leap forward, far removed from good old canned tuna.

*Maguro* is the Japanese word for tuna, the most popular fish for sushi and sashimi in the United States. There are many different kinds of *maguro*, but the four kinds usually used for sushi and sashimi are: blue fin (*hon maguro*), southern blue fin (*minami maguro*), big eye (*mebachi maguro*), and yellow fin (*kiwada*).

Blue fin tuna and southern blue fin are literally the "king of tunas." They are highly prized and expensive. Big eye and yellow fin are somewhat milder in flavor, and are less fatty and less firm in texture. The fattiness is related to size; bigger fish have more fat. In Hawaii these big tunas are called *ahi*.

All four of these kinds of tuna are BIG fish, ranging in weight up to 1,500 pounds for some blue finned varieties, and as much as 300-400 pounds for the big eye and yellow fin. They come from all over the world.

Once a tuna is caught, the head and tail are removed and two large boneless fillets or blocks are cut from either side of the spine. These blocks are called *toro*. The part of the *toro* from the front of the fish is called *otoro*, and it comprises the fattiest, richest part of the fish. Very pale pink in color, it is highly prized and very expensive. Within the front part of this block is a small area called

 *sunazuri*, which is even more succulent. *Sunazuri* is marbled with thin lines of fat and it is considered

to be the "best of the best"!
It is very, very expensive
and not often available in
sushi bars.

The part of the *toro* cut from close to the
tail is called *chutoro*. With its high fat content
and marbled, milky pink color, it too is highly prized and expensive.

The flesh from the top back of the fish is
called *akami,* and it is the sushi grade tuna
that is most often seen in sushi bars and local
fish markets. Dark red and delicious, it is a
much leaner cut.

Since these blocks of fish are sold skinned
and sliced into chunks, it is difficult to tell
which tuna you are buying at a sushi bar or
from your fishmonger. But this is a great
topic to discuss with the *itamae-san*—he
knows! There are many questions to ask:
What kind of tuna is it? Where did it come
from? Has it been frozen? What cut or grade

of tuna is it: *chutoro*, *otoro*, or *akami*? These are also questions to be asked at the fish market. Strictly speaking, only the blue fin tuna is distinguished into *otoro* and *chutoro*, although in reality all of the tunas mentioned are served with these labels.

Other fish served at a sushi bar are somewhat less complicated in terms of their cut. This is mainly due to their size in comparison to tuna. Roundish and flat fish are cut into small fillets. This is also true of *tai* (red snapper), *hamachi* (yellowtail), *sake* (salmon), and other small- to medium-sized fish. It is the back of these fish that works best for sashimi. While in large fish that are eaten raw, such as tuna and swordfish, different parts of the fish have markedly different qualities, mainly in terms of fat content. (which determines color, taste, and texture), these distinctions are not applicable to any significant degree in smaller fish.

The Sushi Menu section of this book (starting on page 56) discusses the many kinds of sashimi (raw fish) that can be used to make sushi.

# OTHER INGREDIENTS— TOPPINGS AND FILLINGS

Rice is always part of any sushi. Fish, shellfish, and fish roe are usually included in most sushi. In addition, lots of other edibles are added to make sushi interesting and varied in taste. For several kinds of sushi, *nori* (a sheet of dried seaweed) is indispensable. Other ingredients that may be included are: fresh vegetables such as cucumber, *daikon* (Japanese white radish), carrot, *negi* (scallions or spring onions), avocado, bean sprouts, *renkon* (lotus root), and mushrooms. Other less familiar ingredients might be *natto* (fermented soybeans), *takuan* (pickled daikon radish), *shiso* (a plant in the mint family), *umeboshi* (pickled Japanese plum, similar to an apricot), and different kinds of seaweed. Tofu and eggs (in the form of omelets) are also used in some kinds of sushi. *Tane* is the word for sushi toppings.

# SUSHI'S BEST FRIENDS—CONDIMENTS

Three condiments are always served with sushi; they add just the right flavor and bite.

**SHOYUN (SOY SAUCE)** is a salty sauce made from soybeans, wheat, malt seed, and yeast that are mixed together and fermented for one year. Lighter and less salty than Chinese soy sauce, it makes a wonderful, necessary addition to sushi and sashimi. It is Japan's most important seasoning.

**GARI (SLICED, PICKLED GINGER)** is made from ginger that has been pickled in salt and sweet vinegar. Salmon pink in color, *gari* is sweet/sour in taste, and a bit crunchy. It is eaten between bites of sushi to refresh and cleanse the palate.

WASABI (JAPANESE HORSERADISH) is an extremely potent horseradish that is not usually available fresh outside of Japan. Powdered wasabi, made from the knobby, green root vegetable, is readily available in the U.S. Mixed with water, it is the best choice for making the thick paste served with sushi. Wasabi is meant to be eaten in very small amounts; it is so pungent that it can literally take your breath away!

If you begin your meal with sashimi, it will be served with wasabi and shredded *daikon*. *Daikon* is far less pungent than other radishes. Mild and crunchy, it is a wonderful accompaniment for sashimi, and it is eaten between bites of fish.

Sushi and sashimi are artistically  arranged on their plates and may be garnished with specially sliced vegetables (or palm leaves or other plant leaves found in Japan) in

the form of flowers, leaves, or fans. These are added to enhance a beautiful presentation or to separate different kinds of sashimi on the same plate. Some decorative garnishes are now made out of plastic.

# MAY I OFFER YOU A DRINK?

*Agari* is tea served with sushi. It was not until the mid 18th century that ordinary people in Japan began to drink green tea (*ocha*) on a regular basis. Of the many grades of green tea, *sencha* is the one most often served with sushi, as it goes particularly well with raw fish. Boiling water is never used to make *sencha*. It should be served piping hot, but if the water is too hot it spoils the flavor of the tea. The tea is steeped for a short time, one minute at the most, and taken without milk, sugar, or lemon. Fine quality green tea leaves and powdered green tea are now available in the U.S. *Sencha* is the perfect beverage to serve with sushi.

SAKE (FERMENTED RICE WINE) is a clear and colorless wine with a fragrant aroma. It has an alcohol content similar to that of most wines, about 15 percent. Fine sake is best served chilled, but warm sake in cold weather is very satisfying. It is the perfect complement to sashimi. Sake does not have the same dulling effect on the taste buds as hard liquor. It enhances flavor and adds to the enjoyment of the meal.

Japan produces 6,000 brands of sake, and each brand includes several different types. This all adds up to an astounding 55,000 choices of rice wine available to the Japanese consumer.

Sake is made from hard rice that is refined and put through a series of processes until it turns into mash. It is allowed to ferment and then mature. The only additives during the fermenting process are yeast and water. Later, alcohol and sugar are added to some grades of sake. When deciding which sake you would like to drink, ask for the advice of your waitress at a sushi bar, or the owner of your favorite wine shop.

BIRU (BEER) goes very well with sushi and can be enjoyed throughout the meal. The fresh, clean taste of beer enhances the taste of sushi. There are several excellent Japanese beers that are always available in sushi bars, including Kirin, which has a rich nutty flavor; Sapporo, which is light and similar to European beer; and Asahi, very much like American beer.

UMESHU (PLUM WINE) is made from *ume* (Japanese apricot). It is not served with sushi, but should be considered as an after-dinner drink. Clear golden brown in color and slightly acidic, yet intensely sweet, it has a wonderful fruity fragrance. Diluted with water and served on the rocks, it makes a satisfying summer drink. It is also served straight as a liqueur.

# the sushi bar

Ahh—the sushi bar! The adventure begins with greetings from the hostess and the chef: *Irasshaimase!* (Welcome!). Most likely, your first visual impression will be of elegant simplicity and order. It is hard to describe how a sense of celebration, including lively conversation and laughter, is combined with a sense of peace and predictability in this ordered place. A sushi bar is in some sense a snack shop, a fast food restaurant, but it is as far from your local McDonald's as you can get. No criticism intended; it's just different, so very different.

# THE ORDER OF THINGS

At the bar you will be seated at a layered counter that is made of wood, probably white cypress. It will be spotlessly clean. Beyond that will be a glass case where the day's carefully prepared fish, shellfish, fish roe, and other delicacies sit on a bed of shaved ice.

At your place there will be a small saucer, a cruet of soy sauce, and *hashi* (wooden chopsticks) in a paper sleeve. Remove the *hashi* from the paper, separate them, and put them down together in front of you. The thin end should be pointing toward the left. It is considered bad luck if they are pointing toward the right. Very soon a waitress will bring you an *oshibori* (a warm or chilled towel, depending on the season) in a basket. You are to wipe your hands and return the towel to the holder. She may pour you some tea. There is usually no charge for this and she will continue to fill your cup throughout the meal. If you need help with anything, she will graciously put you at ease. You will order everything from the waitress except sushi and sashimi. Those things you order from the chef.

Now is the time to order something to drink, typically warm or cooled sake, Japanese beer, or any other beverage you might like. Sake will be served in a small vase-like container. You should fill your partner's sake cup or beer glass, not your own, and the favor should be returned. To receive your drink, hold your cup or glass up in both hands. This gentle custom of thoughtful good manners typifies sushi etiquette.

You may also want some edamame beans (boiled, salted soybeans in the shell) that are fun to pop out of the shells and into your mouth. They are delicious to munch on as you contemplate which sushi to order.

Miso (soybean base) soup, seaweed salad,

or sashimi make nice beginnings. If you order sashimi it will be served artistically arranged, garnished, and accompanied by slivered *daikon* and wasabi. It should be eaten with chopsticks. Put some soy sauce, not too much (that would be impolite!), in your saucer. If you wish, mix with a *little* bit of wasabi. Warning! It is brainfreezingly potent. A little dab'll do ya!

Sake is the perfect accompaniment for sashimi. Since sushi is made with vinegared rice and sake is made from fermented rice, purists do not drink sake with sushi; neither enhances the taste of the other. Many other people don't pay any attention to this notion and continue to drink sake throughout the meal.

# INSIDER TIPS

Most sushi bars do not take reservations for the bar because space is limited, usually not more than 10-15 seats. It is extremely difficult to calculate how long any one given guest will remain at the bar. If you have to wait before being seated, have a beer or sip some sake and enjoy the view.

The best place to sit is definitely at the bar. Try to sit in front of the *itamae-san*, (master chef). This is where the most action takes place. He is the one to ask for suggestions about what to order. What would he recommend? *Omakase*? (chef's choice). Be sure to let him know if you are new at this

and want advice as to what to order. Another reason to try and sit in this spot is that the glass case displaying the fish  may not extend all the way around the bar, and looking at the fish is part of the fun. It is sure to be in front of the *itamae-san*.

The chefs will be working away, preparing sushi delicacies. If it's a first visit and you feel unsure of the protocol, you may decide to go for a table option where you can order a sample plate of sushi, and observe. What you will give up is the feeling of interaction with other diners, the lively conversations that go on with the chef, and his theatrics as he prepares the sushi.

You should order sushi one or two pieces at a time. Once your sushi is served, be sure to notice all the many particulars that make it special—the way it is presented; its arrangement on the plate, which will include wasabi and *gari*; its color, taste, and texture. You should eat it with your fingers, dipping it gently into the soy sauce by tipping the sushi so that the fish or *nori*, not the rice, touch the soy sauce. You don't want to over-season your sushi with soy sauce; which would mask the sushi's delicate blend of flavors. The chef has added a dab of wasabi to the sushi as he prepares it. If you want more wasabi, add it with your chopsticks rather than mixing it into the soy sauce. After each bite of sushi have a bit of *gari* (pickled ginger) to cleanse and refresh your palate.

# Minding Your Manners— Sushi Etiquette

There is something unsettling about being in a social situation in which you sense there are unspoken rules that you don't know. It can make you feel a little uncomfortable, defensive, even flustered. These feelings can crop up at a sushi bar. We all enjoy ourselves more if we know the rules of the game, so let's review some sushi etiquette and helpful tips.

- Don't wash your face with the *oshiboro*; it's for your hands.

- If you have soup, hold the bowl in your hands and sip or slurp the soup from the bowl. Forget everything you ever knew about the polite way to eat soup. While the bowl is close to your mouth, use your chopsticks to pick out any tidbits floating in the soup.

● Remove the *hashi* (wooden chopsticks) from their paper sleeve and separate them. Don't rub them together or play with them. Set them down together in front of you, parallel to the counter's edge, pointing toward the left. Rest them on the *hashi oki* (small holder for chopsticks), the soy saucer, or the paper sleeve that they came in.

# SUSHI 101—
# HELPFUL HINTS

- Eat sashimi with chopsticks, one piece in one bite. Don't drown it in soy sauce, which would overpower the delicate flavor of the fish. Start by ordering blander, white fish first.

- Pour soy sauce into your saucer a little at a time.

- For sashimi you may mix wasabi into the soy sauce. You shouldn't do this for sushi.

- Eat sushi with your fingers, turning it fish side down before dipping it into the soy sauce. If the rice gets wet it may fall apart.

- Although it's customary to eat one whole piece of sashimi in one bite, this is not easy or enjoyable for everyone. An alternative, if one bite is too much, is to take a bite and put the rest back on your plate, unless you can hold the fish in your chopsticks until you are ready for a second bite. Granted, this is not the preferred procedure, but it's the sensible thing to do, since choking is not part of a relaxed dining experience! In the case of sushi, since you are holding it in your hand, it is easy to take a bite and then continue to hold it until you're ready for the next bite.

- Take a small bite of *gari* between bites of sushi to refresh your palate. A bite of *gari*, a sip of tea, and then on to your next bite of sushi—a great combination!

- Ask the waitress, not the chef, for the check.

- Leave a tip on the counter when you depart.

- Relax and have fun.

# WRAPPING THINGS UP

If you have enjoyed the skill and service of the chef you may want to offer him a glass of sake or beer, in recognition of his skill. *Kanpai!* (Cheers!) Whether he accepts it or not, he is sure to appreciate your thoughtfulness. (Remember, drinks are ordered from the waitress.)

For your last round of sushi you may decide to ask for more tea and some *nigiri-zushi* with *tamago-yaki* (a sweetened egg omelet). These two items are often ordered last to signal the end of the meal. When you ask the waitress for the bill, she will get your tally from the chef, who will have kept track of all the sushi you ordered. My guess is that you have had a really good experience, so you will want to leave a generous tip on the counter. *Go chiso sama deshita!* (Thank you very much for the delicious food!)

# THE ITAMAE-SAN

Each sushi bar has an *itamae-san*, gracious artist and performer as well as master chef. Sushi chefs have always been men; this time-honored tradition is still essentially in place. His day begins early in the morning at the market, where he goes to select the freshest, best quality fish (although some of the fish will be frozen). The fish that he buys are whole or in very large pieces. There is much to be done, beginning with scaling, cleaning, and cutting the fish into pieces so they are ready to be sliced for your sushi. He and the other chefs will then attend to all the details of readying the bar before it is opened for business. Once customers arrive, he will be wearing a spotless jacket and a white hat or a *hajimake*, a knotted headband. With his flashing knives and quick hands he will entertain

you as he prepares and presents a wide variety of sushi delicacies.

In Japan, the training of a sushi chef was traditionally a very long process. The training was done by means of an apprenticeship with a master chef. It would last nearly 10 years, and there were no short cuts. It was all about learning self-discipline and self-confidence. The apprentice would begin by doing very humble chores. He would accompany the *itamae-san* to the fish market every day. His job was to carry the fish back to the shop, but also to learn everything there was to know about identifying and purchasing the very best, freshest fish. It was also his job to see that the shop was thoroughly swept and scrubbed until everything was spotlessly clean. He would wash dishes, wash the rice, do random kitchen chores, and make deliveries. This type of work would continue for two to three years. The next step was to learn everything about rice and how to cook and prepare it. This may sound like a simple

 task, but making perfect sushi rice was, and still is, considered to be an art. Then came a more serious concentration on choosing, buying, and preparing fish.

During these years as an apprentice, he would develop a whole host of subtle skills besides those of working with food. He needed to become dignified, gracious, entertaining, confident, and totally in control. Even after this long training it might be years before he would become a head chef. This was a hard-earned profession.

Today's sushi chefs in the United States have had to learn all the same things, but the time devoted to the training period has been considerably shortened. Since the success of a sushi shop depends on the chef, a good chef is much sought after. He will be judged on style as well as skill, and these two qualities can make or break the reputation of a sushi bar. With the proliferation of sushi shops here and all over the world, demand is high for well-trained chefs. Many have not developed the discipline and overall knowledge of the profession, and are referred to as "noodle chefs." They have learned the technical skills of preparing fish, but are lacking in the more subtle qualities of a well-trained sushi chef. Most of us will not know the difference until we have had the opportunity to see a true master chef at work.

# HOW TO USE CHOPSTICKS— AND OTHER TIPS

1. Hold one chopstick in the hollow between your thumb and index finger, resting it on your ring finger.

2. Hold the second chopstick between the tips of your index and middle fingers and your thumb. Manipulate the tip up and down against the tip of the first chopstick, which is held stationary.

3. Get some chopsticks and practice at home.

- Don't pass food from one person to another with chopsticks; this is considered to be bad luck.

- If you are serving food to someone else, turn your chopsticks around and use the thick ends. Use the same technique if you are taking food from a communal platter.

- If you simply can't handle the chopsticks, feel free to ask the waitress for a fork, and you may ask for a spoon for your soup. But asking for a knife is bad manners; it's an insult to the chef and indicates that you think the fish is tough.

# the sushi menu

**K**yo wa nani ga ii desuka? (What's good today?) There will be no menu as you know it. What you will see on the illustrated cards or posters that are displayed at the sushi bar *is* the menu. It is a bewildering display of *nigiri-zushi* (hand-formed sushi or finger sushi), *maki-zushi* (rolled sushi), *temaki-zushi* (coned-shaped, hand-rolled sushi) and *gunkan-maki* (known as battleship roll). *Maki* means roll in Japanese. With luck, Japanese names will be accompanied by English translations. (FYI: the word sushi becomes zushi when it is preceded by a vowel.) Pointing at the items on the menu or fish in the glass case is an acceptable way to request what you want or to find out what is in a particular sushi.

There will be no prices listed. This is because the price and variety of available sushi grade fish changes from day to

day and from season to season. You can be confident that you will not be taken advantage of. The sushi chef will unobtrusively keep track of what and how much you consume. He is trained to do this and it is part of his skill. Fine sushi is, by the way, not inexpensive. You are paying for fresh, pure, and beautifully prepared food. The phrase, "You get what you pay for," certainly applies when you are dealing with raw fish.

When the cowboy was asked what he thought of sushi he responded, "In Texas we call it bait"!

# TYPES OF SUSHI
## WHAT'S ON THE MENU?

● Nigiri-zushi, or finger sushi, is a hand-formed oblong piece of vinegared rice, about 2-1/2 inches x 1 inch, on which the chef puts a dab of wasabi and then a slice of some kind of fish: raw, marinated, or cooked. Wobbly fish are banded on the rice by a thin strip of *nori* called an *obi-jame*.

● Maki-zushi, or rolled sushi, is made by rolling up a layer of rice and selected ingredients in a piece of *nori*. There are several varieties of *maki-zushi*, all similarly prepared but different in size: *Hoso-maki* is a thin, bite-sized version with only one filling besides the rice. *Futo-maki* is a large, fancy roll with more fillings. Since these are meant to be eaten in one or two bites (preferably one) without putting them back on your plate, you might want to ask for *hoso-maki* (one bite)!

*Maki-zushi* ingredients include tuna, scallops, salmon, fish roe, avocado, cucumber, *umeboshi,* scallions, spicy salmon skin, shrimp, spicy crab, freshwater eel, and many others, combined in interesting ways.

● Putting rice and other fillings in a piece of nori and rolling it up into the shape of a cone makes temaki-zushi, or hand-rolled sushi. The ingredients for *temaki* are similar to those for *maki-zushi.*

● Gunkan-maki, or battleship roll sushi, is made with rice hand-formed into an oblong shape and surrounded by an upright 1-inch x 6-inch strip of *nori* to form a "boat." It is usually filled with fish or fish roe.

# WHAT'S NOT ON THE MENU?

Besides the four types of sushi listed above, there are several others that may not be on the menu, but are usually available on request. They are:

● Ura-maki is known as an inside-out roll. Various ingredients, including a sheet of *nori*, are rolled up with a layer of rice on the outside and sliced into several pieces. The rice is often sprinkled with black or white toasted sesame seeds or flying fish roe. The ingredients for making *ura-maki* are the same as those used for *maki-zushi*, using no more than two items besides the rice.

● Oshi-zushi, or pressed sushi, evolved from the ancient custom of packing salted fish and rice together to preserve the fish. Today, rice and other ingredients are pressed together in a small mold. When they are removed from the mold they are cut into bite-sized pieces. Some of the popular types of *oshi-zushi* are made with vinegared mackerel, shrimp, freshwater eel, sea bass, and *shiso* (perilla leaves).

● Chirashi-zushi, which means scattered sushi, is the easiest sushi to prepare and can have any combination of toppings. It is a one-dish meal! A bowl of sushi rice is topped with combinations of fish, vegetables, tofu, or egg omelet. The result, with toppings artistically arranged on the rice, can be a work of art.

● Inari-zushi is made with a special kind of packaged deep fried tofu, which forms pouches or pockets when cut in half. The tofu, filled with sushi rice, is sweet and tasty. It can also be mixed with finely chopped vegetables, bits of fish, toasted sesame seeds, lemon zest, or other combinations of ingredients. If it is available at a sushi bar the chef may suggest his own specialty.

In Japanese mythology, foxes are the messengers of Inari, the god of agriculture. They guard the shrines of Inari. Since *Inari-zushi* has pointed corners that resemble fox ears, this sushi was named for these envoys of Inari. A favorite food of Japanese foxes is fried tofu, and it is left for them to eat near the shrines of Inari, thus reinforcing the association.

All these sushi offerings are served accompanied by wasabi and *gari*.

# TYPES OF SASHIMI (AND NIGIRI-ZUSHI)

Let's take a look at the menu, starting with the *nigiri-zushi* offerings. Listed below are the names of the most commonly offered types of sashimi (raw fish), as well as some fish that are cooked or prepared in other ways before serving. Since you order *nigiri-zushi* by the name of the fish that tops the rice, this sashimi list is also a list of *nigiri-zushi*.

One cannot expect to remember all the names and descriptions in the following reference. The best thing to do is to talk to the chef, ask what he recommends, and what the specials are. It is the chef's job to help, entertain, and serve you with utmost grace—and you can expect that he will. Remember, you can always point! For first timers, I suggest trying *maguro* (tuna), *sake* (salmon), *unagi* (fresh water eel), and *ebi* (shrimp).

● Maguro *tuna*

COLOR: deep red
TASTE: delicate, sweet, clean
TEXTURE: meaty, smooth, soft

● Chutoro *tuna from the belly*

COLOR: milky pink, marbled
TASTE: rich, high fat content
TEXTURE: very tender and buttery
NOTE: expensive

● Otoro *tuna from the front belly*

COLOR: pale pink
TASTE: rich, very high fat content
TEXTURE: extraordinarily "melt-in-the-mouth" tender
NOTE: very expensive

● Hamachi *young yellowtail*

COLOR: light golden, may display a dark streak along its edges
TASTE: slightly fatty, bold smoky taste, tangy aftertaste
TEXTURE: buttery, yet firm

## ● Makajiki *swordfish*

COLOR: creamy white with some red delineation

TASTE: delicate, somewhat fatty

TEXTURE: firm

NOTE: There is currently some concern about high levels of mercury in swordfish. It is worth checking recent FDA and EPA recommendations.

## ● Kohada *shad, sometimes called gizzard shad*

COLOR: white flesh, silver skin speckled with black dots

TASTE: strong intense flavor

TEXTURE: soft, chewy

NOTE: *Kohada*, usually imported from Japan, is marinated in vinegar to soften its many small bones. The silvery skin is scored before serving.

## ● Saba *mackerel*

COLOR: bands of light and dark flesh

TASTE: strong, salty, insistent

TEXTURE: firm, oily

NOTE: *Saba* is usually salted and marinated before being served. It must be put on ice within hours of being caught or its flavor deteriorates. Saba is usually flown in from Japan. It is best in the autumn.

## ● Sake *salmon*

COLOR: bright orange

TASTE: delicate, sweet

TEXTURE: meltingly tender, succulent

NOTE: Wild salmon is best because of its diet of crustaceans, which results in its vibrant color and rich flavor. In Japan it is never eaten raw because of the parasites present in Japanese salmon. In the U.S. it is eaten raw, but should first be frozen.

● Tai *red snapper, porgy*

COLOR: pink and white, skin is often left on
TASTE: sweet, delicate, pleasant bite
TEXTURE: lean, firm
NOTE: Japanese *tai*, red sea bream, is not available in the U.S. You may be served red snapper, porgy, flounder, fluke, or other white fish with the same attributes. Ask the chef exactly which fish is being served.

● Hirame *halibut*

COLOR: pale pink, translucent
TASTE: delicate flavor
TEXTURE: dense, can be slightly crunchy
NOTE: Wonderful when sliced paper thin for sashimi and served with ponzu sauce (citrus flavored soy sauce made with rice wine vinegar, sweet sake, sugar, and citrus). Best December to January.

● Suzuki *sea bass*

COLOR: shiny white
TASTE: mild, delicate flavor
TEXTURE: broad-flaked and firm
NOTE: best in summer months

● Unagi *freshwater eel*

COLOR: nut brown
TASTE: rich, smoky
TEXTURE: tender, succulent
NOTE: Freshwater eel is never served raw; it is filleted and steamed. Before serving it is glazed with *tare* (a sweet, smoky sauce made of sugar, soy sauce, and eel broth) and grilled. Since it has already been seasoned, this delicacy should not be dipped in soy sauce. This is a very popular, tasty fish and a good choice for a first time sushi diner.

On the Day of the Cow or Ox, everyone in Japan eats eel. The idea is that eating eel on this day, which falls during the summer solstice, will ensure good health for the whole year. The Japanese embrace this tradition so enthusiastically that more than 850 tons of *unagi* are eaten on this day every year! It is also supposed to enhance one's love life! It is sometimes served to newlyweds for their first breakfast together.

● Anago *salt water eel*

COLOR: golden

TASTE: rich, smoky

TEXTURE: less fatty, less tender, thus less sought after than *unagi* (see page 69).

● Tako *octopus*

COLOR: white, edged by burgundy red after slicing

TASTE: sweet, clean, mild

TEXTURE: firm with a bit of a resistance to the bite

NOTE: Octopus is always boiled, which tenderizes the meat and causes the tentacles to curl and become firm and the flesh to become opaque.

● Ika *squid*

COLOR: pearly, faintly pink or white

TASTE: tastes of the sea, with a slight iodine flavor

TEXTURE: springy, a bit rubbery, yet tender

● Awabi *abalone*

COLOR: peach or gray flesh

TASTE: mild

TEXTURE: chewy

NOTE: The abalone is a large sea snail. As sashimi, the edible "foot" is served thinly sliced and scored.

● Ikura *salmon roe*

COLOR: shiny, translucent, bright orange

TASTE: slightly salty

TEXTURE: About the size of peas, when fresh the flavorful eggs "pop" in your mouth. When not fresh, *ikura* is soggy, and smells and tastes too "fishy."

## ● Uni *sea urchin roe*

COLOR: mustard yellow

TASTE: mild, nutty flavor

TEXTURE: soft, smooth texture

NOTE: When fresh, *uni* is a choice delicacy for the connoisseur; however, it is an acquired taste. Very expensive.

## ● Tobiko *flying fish roe*

COLOR: bright orange, the size of a grain of sand

TASTE: mild, salty/sweet flavor

TEXTURE: crunchy texture; the flavor bursts in your mouth when you bite them.

## Kazunoko *herring roe*

COLOR: tiny white eggs marinated in sweet sake, broth, and soy sauce, which give them a golden yellow color

TASTE: delicate, slightly salty flavor resulting from the marinade

TEXTURE: crunchy

NOTE: The eggs are so "packed" together that they are often sliced en masse. They are so expensive that they are referred to as "yellow diamonds." *Kazunoko* is a traditional Japanese New Year's Eve dish.

## Mirugai *large horseneck clam*

COLOR: pale peach

TASTE: subtle shellfish flavor

TEXTURE: rubbery, chewy

NOTE: It is the muscular siphon that is served as sushi; not to everyone's taste.

● Kobashira *small scallops*
  Kaibashira *small scallops*

(Scallops in general are called *hotategai*.)

COLOR: white

TASTE: delicately sweet

TEXTURE: melt-in-your-mouth tender

NOTE: For sushi, the large, white adductor muscle is used. The Japanese refer to the adductor muscle of all clams as scallops. Can be eaten fresh, dry frozen, or marinated for subtle flavor.

● Kaki *oysters*

COLOR: grey

TASTE: salty flavor

TEXTURE: watery, slidhery

● Kani kama *imitation crab*

COLOR: red/orange and white

TASTE: tasty, familiar flavor

TEXTURE: firm

NOTE: always cooked for sushi

● Ama ebi *raw shrimp and prawns*

COLOR: glossy, somewhat transparent, grey or pink jewel-like color

TASTE: sweet

TEXTURE: tender

NOTE: This delicacy is sometimes served with the head deep-fried. It must be of very special quality and is thus not readily available.

● Ebi *cooked shrimp and prawns*

COLOR: striped white and pink/orange

TASTE: familiar, delicate flavor

TEXTURE: firm

NOTE: *Ebi* are usually split into butterfly shapes before serving.

● Tamago-yaki *hen egg omelet*

COLOR: light yellow

TASTE: sweet, flavored with sugar, salt, sake and mirin (sweet wine)

TEXTURE: moist and firm

NOTE: Made in a special rectangular pan in which the chef creates firm, paper-thin layers to a depth of about one inch. When served as topping for *nigiri-zushi*, it is banded by an *obi-jame* (thin *nori* belt or strip).

Gambling dens used to be known as *tekka*. Gangsters and other shady characters played cards in these establishments, where they would order take-out sushi so they could eat without stopping the game. However, the rice would stick to their fingers and then to the cards, making it easy for them to cheat by marking their cards with sticky rice. This was a problem. They decided to ask to have *nori* wrapped around the sushi, which would eliminate the "sticky" problem. Wanting a little more taste, they requested that a bit of tuna be put in the roll. Voila, the first *tekka-maki!*

# OTHER MENU ITEMS

The other items that will be pictured on the "menu" at the sushi bar are *maki-zushi*, *temaki-zushi* (hand-rolled, cone-shaped sushi), and *gunkan-maki* (*nori*-wrapped "boat" sushi, usually filled with roe).

## TYPES OF MAKI-ZUSHI

Some popular kinds of *maki-zushi*, the sliced rolls of filled *nori* that are a sushi staple:

TEKKA: raw tuna
NEGI-TORO: tuna belly and scallions
UNAKYU: grilled freshwater eel and cucumber
ANAKYU: grilled marine eel and cucumber
SABAGARI: mackerel, ginger, and cucumber
SAKEKAWA: salmon skin and cucumber
EBIKYU: shrimp, cucumber, and fish roe

NEGIHAMACHI: mackerel and scallions

CALIFORNIA ROLL: shrimp, crabstick, cucumber, and avocado (in some combination)

UMEBOSHI: pickled plum (Japanese apricot)

UMEKYU: pickled plum (Japanese apricot) and cucumber

OSHINKO: pickled *daikon* (white radish)

KAPPA: cucumber

There is a Japanese myth about a water goblin named Kappa. He loved cucumbers and stole them from people who lived along the riverbanks. Pictures of Kappa always show him with a little bowl on his head that looks like a slice of cucumber. *Kappa maki* is named after this pesky little goblin.

# KANPAI!
# (TO YOUR HEALTH!)

Now that you have perused the menu and decided what you would like to eat, there are a few other things that you should know about ordering. It is customary to ask the chef for one or two orders of sushi at a time. *Nigiri-zushi* is always served in pairs; one order is two pieces. If you ask for two that means two orders and you will get four pieces. This is not so with *maki-zushi*. With rolled sushi, one order is one roll and it is cut into several slices. If you order *nigiri-zushi* and *maki-zushi* at the same time you should eat the *maki-zushi* first. (The *nori* should be eaten right away so that it will remain crisp and easier to eat.)

All this may seem like a bit much just for a tasty little dinner, but really it isn't. It's just a new experience, let's say a cultural adventure. The learning curve may seem a bit daunting if you haven't been to a sushi bar before. But once you get the hang of it, you will revel in the taste of the food, the performance of the chef, the artistic presentation, and the graciousness of the staff. Last but not least, you will celebrate your own growing expertise in mastering the "know hows" of this special dining experience. If you already have, you know what I mean.

# SUSHI TALK—
# WHY NOT GIVE IT A TRY?

IRASSHAIMASE: welcome

KONNICHIWA: hello (in the afternoon)

KONBANWA: Good evening

IIE: no

SUMIMASEN: excuse me

OMAKASE: chef's choice

SABINUKI: no wasabi, please

OISHII: delicious

KANPAI: cheers, to your health

ITADAKIMASU: bon appetit, I receive/accept with thanks

DOMO: thank you

GO CHISO SAMA DESHITA: thank you very much for the delicious meal

ARIGATO: thanks

OKANJO: bill, check

ARIGATO GOZAIMASHITA: thank you very much (at the end of the evening)

OYASUMI NASAI: good night

# becoming your own
# sushi chef

Making sushi can be relatively simple or very complicated. Learning some basic facts, like how to handle the very sticky, sticky rice, will make the process easier. Besides some basic equipment for making the sushi, you will need to choose the ingredients that seem tasty and suitable, as well as available, for making sushi at home. As you become more skilled you will want to try more types of sushi and interesting new fillings.

The easiest types of sushi to make are *chirashi-zushi* (scattered), *oshi-zushi* (pressed) and *temaki-zushi* (hand-rolled). For these three types of sushi, only the minimum of equipment is needed and no special skills are

required. It is a good idea to start your career as a sushi chef by making these simple types of sushi.

Since *nigiri-zushi* and *maki-zushi* are sushi bar favorites, you may be tempted to start with them. The sushi chef, after all, makes them look so easy! Well it's the old "looks can be deceiving" thing. *Nigiri-zushi* is said to be the most difficult type of sushi to make, requiring a gentle touch and a mastery of rice. Making *maki-zushi* is also not so easy. It requires special equipment, a tender touch, and an experienced eye to roll just the right amount of filling in such a way that the *nori* doesn't split, the rice doesn't come squishing out all over everything, and the roll sticks together. That being said, don't worry! You *are* going to learn to make all the kinds of sushi on the menu. It just takes a little patience and lots of practice. Begin with simple sushi, and work into the more difficult types as you learn. Success with simpler tasks is better than getting discouraged right from the "get-go." So relax, have fun, and before long you'll be hosting your own sushi party.

# TOOLS OF THE TRADE— EQUIPPING YOUR KITCHEN

### ● Hangiri *rice-cooling tub*

A *hangiri* is made of wood, usually cypress, and banded with wide copper strips. It has low sides and a flat bottom, which speeds the cooling process. Sushi rice is placed in it to be seasoned and cooled after it is cooked. Its flat

bottom makes it easier to fold in the vinegar mixture. It provides the right conditions for the rice to acquire the appropriate texture and gloss. Covered by a damp cloth, the rice is kept in the *hangiri* until it is ready to be used for sushi.

### ● Shamoji *wooden rice paddle*

A *shamoji* is a broad flat paddle used to fold

seasoning into the rice and to gently spread and turn over the rice as it cools. It's a good idea to soak the *shamoji* in cold water before using so the rice doesn't stick to it. A wooden spoon or spatula may be substituted for the *shamoji*.

## ● Uchiwa *fan*

An *uchiwa* is a flat fan made of bamboo ribs covered with either paper or silk. If you do not have this kind of fan, a piece of heavy paper or cardboard, or an electric fan, can be used instead. Fanning the rice encourages the evaporation of moisture and is crucial to giving it the right texture and flavor.

## ● Zaru *bamboo strainer*

The traditional bamboo colander was used to wash and drain the rice before it was cooked. Now the Japanese use metal colanders specifically for draining rice; they are called *kome-agezaru*. Any metal or plastic colander can be used for this purpose if it has a fine drain.

### ● Hocho *knives*

Serrated stainless-steel knives should not be used for making sushi. They will tear rather than make clean cuts. One should use good quality, very sharp steel knives. A sushi chef wields his knives with such speed and skill that it is a pleasure to watch him in action. They are the tools of his trade. There are two types of knives that you should have for making sushi:

### ● Usuba-bocho *vegetable knife*

This knife has a long blade, which is broad and oblong. It is used to peel, cut, and chop vegetables and other non-fish ingredients of sushi.

### ● Sashimi-bocho *fish slicing knife*

This knife is used for slicing fish and cutting sushi. It is a long pointed knife, which can

also be used for making garnishes.

● Makisu *bamboo rolling mat*

This mat is used for making rolled sushi. It is made of bamboo sticks held together by cotton string. There is no substitute for this mat; you must have it. They come in various sizes, but the most versatile is 9-1/2 inches square.

● Oshibako *pressed sushi mold*

These molds are traditionally made of cypress wood, and come in many different sizes. Each mold has a removable top and bottom to facilitate the pressing together of rice and other ingredients. Plastic pressed-sushi molds are now available. They are easy to use and quick to clean. Other things can be used to make pressed sushi. For instance, cookie cutters lined with plastic wrap or rinsed in vinegared water make interesting shapes and are fun to use when making sushi for children.

## ● Chopping Board

You will need at least one chopping board for slicing raw fish, vegetables, and rolled sushi. Either wooden or plastic boards are suitable. It's not a bad idea to have one for each kind of slicing job. If you are using one board, be sure to wash it thoroughly and dry it between different uses. If it is used for anything involving rice, rinse the board in lightly vinegared water and pat it slightly dry so the rice won't stick to the board.

TIP: Any utensil that is made of wood should be thoroughly washed and dried after using. Leave it out overnight to dry completely. It should be stored in a dry place so that it does not become moldy.

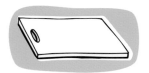

# THE GROCERY— STOCKING YOUR KITCHEN

Since the right rice and freshest fish are the keys to great sushi, they should be on the top of your grocery list.

## THE RICE

The rice you should choose for making sushi is premium quality Japanese or California short grain rice. It is available in most supermarkets and in all Japanese or Asian markets. It clings together and has just the right chewy consistency. Its color and sheen, if prepared properly, are right on target. Pay close attention to the instructions for making sushi rice.

## THE FISH

Locate a first rate fishmonger who is accustomed to selling sushi or sashimi grade fish.

Instead of scaling, skinning and filleting whole fish yourself, buy blocks or fillets of sushi grade fish that are prepared by the fishmonger. However, it is a good idea to look carefully at the whole fish displayed in the shop to see how fresh they are. If they meet your standards, you can be pretty well assured that the fillets and blocks of fish will also be of high quality.

## MEASURES OF FRESHNESS:

- The fish should smell clean and fresh, not "fishy."

- The fish should be firm and springy to the touch.

- The underside of the gills should be red or pink, and moist.

- The eyes should look clear, not cloudy.

- Scales should be attached and shiny.

- The skin of the fish should have some luster.

Finding fresh fish roe to use in sushi can be difficult. If your fish market does not have them, ask if they can be ordered. Bottled fish roe is available in most markets, sometimes referred to as caviar. If you check around you will probably locate some kind of fish roe to use for *gunkan-maki* and for the finishing touch on other sushi.

Buy only live shellfish. The shells will probably be tightly closed. If they are open and you tap the shell, they should close up. Open shells that do not close up mean that the shellfish is dead. Shells should be free of cracks and nicks. Scallops should smell fresh. They will have been shucked and are sold wet or dry. Wet means that they have been treated to look better and be appealing for a longer time. Dry scallops are in their natural form and taste much better; they must be fresh. Ask how long it has been since they were shucked.

Tell the fishmonger that you will be using the fish for sushi. Ask him some questions. Where did the fish come from? Were they previously frozen? When were they delivered? What days does he receive deliveries of fresh fish? Is it possible to special order fish in the future? Get to know him; he may have tips and interesting stories to tell about sushi and fish in general.

Frozen fish from a fish market is also a good option. The freezing completely removes any worry about parasites. They should be frozen solid, with no freezer burn. Frozen fish that the market receives have been flash frozen at an extremely low temperature almost immediately after being caught and/or dressed.

Most fish that are displayed already filleted are not suitable for sushi. For small- to medium-sized fish, I recommend buying the whole fish and asking the fishmonger to

 fillet and de-bone it for you. Tuna or salmon already in chunks or fillets, if they are sushi grade, are acceptable to buy in this form. They should be firm in texture and somewhat translucent, with no liquid around them. They should smell clean, not fishy. Tuna belly should be light red in color and display visible stripes. Other parts of the tuna should be clear red. Never buy packaged fish for sushi.

Since there is a risk of health complications if you eat raw fish that is not really fresh, has not been frozen, or that has not been handled properly, I recommend serving only the following raw fish at home. Let's call them "first fish." Once you are well acquainted with your fishmonger, you may decide to add some others to those you feel comfortable serving at home.

First fish include tuna, flounder, scallops, clams, and oysters. Other good choices which have already been cooked or otherwise pre-pared are shrimp, smoked salmon (or other smoked fish), crabmeat, artificial crabmeat, squid, octopus, and freshwater eel.

Another option for acquiring fine sushi grade fish is to check with local sushi bars to see if they would sell you some. You may be able to buy fish in blocks or fillets. Their fish would be of the best quality and would likely offer the most variety to choose from. It's worth a try.

# BRINGING IN THE HAUL

Pick up the fish the day you intend to eat it, the closer to serving time the better. Bring a cooler containing crushed ice to the market. Place the wrapped fish on top of one layer of ice and cover it with more ice. Containers of shellfish should have holes because the shellfish will be alive and will need some air. Once home, place the fish, on ice, in the bottom of the refrigerator (that's usually the coldest spot). Since the ice will gradually melt, make sure to put it in some sort of container. If the fish is frozen it should be thawed in the refrigerator, which will take at least five hours. You could also thaw it overnight, the day before you intend to serve it. Wrap it loosely in plastic wrap and put in a dish to catch the liquid that will result from the thawing process.

# Keeping Things Clean

Be sure to wash your hands with hot soapy water and rinse with ice cold water before handling raw fish. You should do this with all the equipment that will come in contact with the fish. Rinse the fish in lightly salted cold water before preparing it for sushi. Warm hands, warm water, or warm kitchen utensils can negatively affect the quality of the fish. Handling can bruise the fish, so be gentle.

All this may sound ultra cautious, but it is always better to be safe than sorry. Think about it—how often have you eaten raw fish, besides perhaps shellfish, at home? This is a new adventure and you need to do things the right way. This is how the chefs at a sushi bar choose and handle the fish, and wash their hands and tools. Since you are a sushi chef in training, you should too!

# DRY THINGS

AGARI or OCHA—is tea. *Sencha* is the green tea most often served with sushi. It is made either with tea leaves or powder made from the leaves.

GOMA—are black or white sesame seeds. They are wonderful when toasted.

KATSUOBUSHI—are dried bonito flakes used for making soup stock.

KOMBU—are dark green leaves of dried kelp, used to flavor sushi rice.

NORI—is seaweed that has been made into thin sheets. It is used to make many types of sushi.

WAKAME—is dried seaweed. When reconstituted, *wakame* is chewy, smooth, and wonderfully sweet.

WASABI—is very pungent Japanese horse-radish. The powdered form allows you to make just as much as you will be using at any one time, whereas the wasabi in tubes must be refrigerated after opening and will not keep very long.

# THINGS IN BOTTLES

MIRIN—is syrupy sweet sake used only for cooking.

MISO—is salty, fermented soybean paste. It comes in different grades in terms of saltiness. *Shiro-miso* is light, *aka-miso* is medium, and *kuro-miso* is the strongest. They are used in miso soup. Miso is sold in cellophane or plastic packages.

SAKE—is Japanese rice wine, which is used for cooking and as a beverage.

SHOYU—is Japanese soy sauce. Lighter than Chinese soy sauce, it is more suited as an accompaniment for sushi.

SU—is Japanese rice vinegar.

# VEGGIES

Asparagus, avocado, carrots, spring onions or chives, mushrooms, radishes, snow peas, sprouts, watercress, dill, capers, and other familiar vegetables can all be used in creative ways when making sushi.

DAIKON—is a large, white, mild-tasting Japanese radish.

EDAMAME—are soybeans in their pods. They are slightly larger than peas. They're tasty, healthful, and fun to eat. You strip the beans out of the pod with your teeth or fingers. They can also be purchased shelled, and you can find them in the freezer at the market.

JAPANESE CUCUMBER—has thin tasty skin, very few seeds, and is not watery, which makes it an excellent crunchy sushi ingredient. If it is not available in your area, substitute with the greenhouse or English variety of cucumber.

RENKON—is lotus root. Once sliced, it displays an attractive, lacy look. It adds crunch to any rolled sushi. First peeled and sliced, it is then soaked and briefly cooked in vinegared water.

SHISO LEAF (OR PERILLA)—is an attractive, aromatic, tasty leaf, which is a member of the mint family, but tastes a bit like basil.

## PICKLED THINGS

GARI—is sweet and sour, crunchy pickled ginger, a refreshing palate cleanser between bites of sushi.

TAKUAN—is a soft, crunchy pickled *daikon* radish. Delicious in taste and delightful in color, it is bright yellow.

UMEBOSHI—is pickled unripe Japanese plums or apricots. It has a salty, acidic taste. Once the pits are removed, the plums are cut up for accents of taste and color in different kinds of rolled sushi.

# OTHER TASTY THINGS

ABURA-AGE—is deep-fried tofu, which can be stuffed to make *inari-zushi*. Sliced up, it is used in other kinds of sushi as well. It can be found in Asian markets.

DASHI—There are several varieties of this Japanese soup stock, which is used as a base for many dishes, including the recipes in this book for *inari-zushi* and miso soup.

KANI KAMA—is imitation crabmeat that is made out of pollock, and is a tasty and convenient ingredient for *maki-zushi*, *ura-maki-zushi*, and *temaki-zushi*.

TOFU—is soybean curd. It is very nutritious, high in protein, and low in fat and sugar. Japanese tofu is smooth and creamy, and is sold in Asian markets. If it is not available in your area, buy silken tofu at your grocery store. It makes a nice addition, cut into small cubes, to miso soup.

# recipes and tips

# IMPORTANT TIPS FOR SUSHI SUCCESS

● Keep your sushi kitchen as clean and neat as possible. Don't let raw fish get mixed up with anything else.

● Have all ingredients that you will need prepared and at the ready.

● To ensure the best results, handle the rice as gently as possible. Don't squeeze it or press down on it with force. When compacting it, use firm, even pressure.

● Try not to overstuff any rolled sushi. If you do, the rice will squish out all over the place, the *nori* will split—and you will be very frustrated.

● Most important! Whenever you are going to handle rice, you *must* rinse your hands in a mixture of vinegar and water (1/4 cup rice vinegar to 1 cup water). That means every single time! After dipping your hands in the water, tap them lightly on a hand towel, which you should keep next to the water/vinegar mixture. You don't want your hands to be dripping wet, just moist.

● If the rice should get out of control and starts to get all over you and everything else, stop and clean it up before proceeding. Trust me on this; the rice seems to take on a life of its own!

● Keep a hand towel well dampened with the vinegar/water mixture to wipe your knives on before or between cuts involving rice.

● It is best to place sushi on clean, smooth surfaces.

● Anything made of wood should be damp before it comes in contact with the rice.

And now let's make some different kinds of sushi. Good luck!

# SLICING SASHIMI

The knife you need for making sushi is a *sashimi-bocho*, used for slicing fish. Investing in a really good quality knife will make cutting easier, not only in sushi making, but also for regular cooking tasks. The knife should be very sharp. You will be surprised how much easier it is to do any kind of slicing or cutting job with a really sharp knife. You will also need a cutting board. Wooden boards are best, but plastic boards are easier to keep clean.

A vegetable knife, a *usuba-bocho*, is also important to have in your sushi kitchen. The same advice applies as for your *sashimi-bocho*: razor sharpness is essential! Usually, you will be using a straight cut with this knife. Let the blade do the work. Sharp is the key word in describing a fine knife, but be careful with it!

It is not within the scope of this book to discuss the process of dressing whole fish. The instructions that follow assume that you have obtained fresh or frozen blocks or fillets of sushi grade fish from your fishmonger.

The way you slice your fish depends on the type of sushi you are making. For *nigiri-zushi*, the fish is cut across the grain into thin diagonal slices. These slices are then cut into "sticks" for *maki-zushi* and *temaki-zushi*. For pressed sushi, larger, flatter slices are ideal. Scattered sushi requires smaller, uniform slices.

## How to hold your knife and make the desired cuts

Hold the fish knife firmly by the handle, with your index finger extending slightly onto the blade. Use gentle pressure; a very sharp knife does most of the work for you. You need only guide the knife, either through the fish on an angle along the length of the blade, or by pressing directly down on the blade to make a straight cut. Straight cutting is used to cut

 larger pieces of fish into a size that can then be sliced into topping or filling for sushi. You will not be cutting through skin and bone so you will not need a cleaver.

For a right-handed person, the fish being cut is always held with the left hand on the left end of the fish. (Left-handers should reverse these instructions.) Your hand will be between the end of the fish and the knife blade. The cut is usually made on the side of the block or fillet—that is, across the grain.

For thin diagonal slices, holding the fish gently with the left hand, and the knife at a 45-degree angle, draw the blade of the knife across and through the fish, producing even slices of the desired width. The first slice will have less of a uniform shape than the ones that follow, as it establishes the degree of slant that is needed. This can be used for kinds of sushi in which the shape won't matter.

For hand-rolled and other rolled sushi, follow the same procedure as above, making the slices slightly thicker. You then cut the slices into sticks of the desired length.

Slices for pressed sushi are made in a similar way, the difference being that the cut starts further from the edge of the fish and the blade is angled only slightly, almost parallel to the cutting surface. The slices should be as thin as possible. This is also the way to cut whitefish and other flat fillets for sashimi and sushi.

For *chirashi-zushi*, slightly thicker, less angled slices are made, and then these slices are straight cut from the top to make uniform pieces the right size for arranging artistically on the rice.

# SUSHI RICE (SUMESHI)

To make the *sumeshi* you will need a large, heavy-bottomed pan with a tight-fitting lid, a wooden *hangiri* (Japanese wooden rice-cooling tub), a *shamo-ji* (broad wooden spatula) for mixing the dressing into the rice, and an *uchiwa* (paper fan) with which to cool the rice. That being said, you can, of course, improvise. A large, nonmetallic flat-bottomed bowl can be used for the cooked rice. A wooden spatula can take the place of a paddle, and you can use whatever is available for a fan, such as a piece of cardboard or a magazine. For those willing to invest in an electric rice cooker, the whole process is simpler and takes all the guesswork

out of making perfect rice. Sushi chefs tend to have their own "secret recipes" for the vinegar dressing used to make *sumeshi*, but they all use some combination of rice vinegar, sugar, and salt, to which they may add a little something to make their rice the "best."

Read the recipe through before you begin.

*1-3/4 cups Japanese short grain rice*
*2 cups cold water*
*3-inch x 5-inch piece kombu (seaweed)*
*1 tablespoon sake (optional—added to make the rice extra plump!)*
*3 tablespoons rice vinegar*
*2 1/2 tablespoons sugar*
*2 teaspoons salt*

In a sieve, wash the rice thoroughly by submerging in cold water in a large bowl. Throw away the milky water and repeat until the water is clear. Drain and let the rice sit in the sieve for 30 minutes.

Soak the wooden bowl (with wooden paddle inside) in cool water. Immerse the

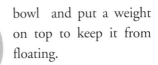 bowl and put a weight on top to keep it from floating.

Clean the *kombu* (seaweed) with a damp cloth and make several cuts in one side.

Put the rice into a large, heavy-bottomed saucepan; add the cold water, *kombu*, and sake (optional). Cover and bring to a boil over high heat. Once the water boils, remove the *kombu* and re-cover. Lower the heat to medium and cook for 5 minutes.

Reduce the heat to low and simmer until the water is absorbed, about 10-15 minutes. Remove from heat. Remove lid, spread a clean kitchen towel over the top of the pot, then replace the lid and let stand for 15 minutes to finish cooking.

While the rice is cooking, prepare the vinegar dressing. Combine vinegar, sugar, and salt in a small non-aluminum saucepan.

Heat slowly until the sugar and salt have dissolved. Stir constantly, not allowing the mixture to boil. Remove from heat and set aside to cool.

Remove the wooden bowl from the water and wipe dry.

Once the rice has been off the stove for 15 minutes, empty it into the wooden bowl and spread it evenly over the bottom with the wooden paddle. Use a horizontal slicing motion to separate the grains. Begin to add the vinegar mixture to the rice, a little at a time, continuing the slicing motion to coat the grains of rice. If the mixture seems to get at all mushy at any point, don't add any more liquid. At the same time, if you can manage all this at once, fan the rice to cool it. (A helper would be a wonderful thing to have at this point!) Continue adding the vinegar mixture, and cooling until the

rice begins to look glossy and has cooled to room temperature. This whole process should take about 10 minutes.

Cover the bowl with a damp kitchen towel, and keep in a cool spot in your kitchen until ready to use. Do not refrigerate!

MAKES FOUR CUPS (1 QUANTITY)

Wow! At this moment you're probably wondering about how much a nice little rice cooker would cost. Or maybe about whether you could use an electric fan to cool the rice. (That would be OK.) Anyway, congratulations—you did it!

Remember, as mentioned earlier: it is crucial to rinse your hands in vinegared water every time you handle the rice.

# CHIRASHI-ZUSHI

The easiest sushi to make is scattered sushi, a kind of "sushi salad." Basically, it consists of a bowl of sushi rice with a variety of ingredients on top of, or mixed into, the rice. It is a meal in itself. The two types of *chirashi-zushi* are Tokyo style (*edomae-chirashi-zushi*) and Kansai style (*gomoko-chirashi-zushi*). Tokyo style is a bowl of rice topped with one or several kinds of *sashimi*. The sashimi is artfully arranged and garnished. In Kansai style the ingredients are cooked or raw, and mixed into the rice. The top of the rice is decoratively garnished.

Another type of *chirashi-zushi* is save-the-day-*chirashi-zushi* (my own invention). This type of sushi happens when you are preparing another kind of sushi and something goes terribly wrong. You become

flexible and inventive. You rename what you are making and it becomes your own special *chirashi-zushi*. Nothing is lost, just "recreated." If you proceed with cheerful confidence, no one will be the wiser. Just mix or rearrange the ingredients, slice and snip, add anything you wish, and then garnish with a radish rose and a smile.

# FLOWER PETAL CHIRASHI-ZUSHI

*1 quantity (4 cups) sushi rice*
*8 ounces tuna or salmon sashimi*
*8 ounces flounder sashimi*
*2 tablespoons* gari
*Watercress leaves for garnish*
*Wasabi*

Place rice into four bowls and set on plates. Slice each kind of fish into eight 1/2-inch pieces, then cut each of these slices in half (a total of 32 pieces of fish). Arrange the fish as petals, in a circle around each rice bowl center, with red (tuna) on one half and white (flounder) on the other half, forming a flower. Place a dab of wasabi and some *gari* in the center of the "flower." Tuck a few watercress leaves here and there, around the outside edge.

SERVES 4

# FRUIT SALAD
# CHIRASHI-ZUSHI

The combination of the tangy
sweet/sour rice and the sweet taste of
the fruit is very pleasing to the palate.
This is an unusual, refreshing kind of
*chirashi-zushi*.

*1 cup blueberries*
*1 cup strawberries*
*1 cup mango*
*Mint leaves*
*1 quantity (4 cups) sushi rice*

Wash and dry fruit. Slice strawberries in half
and cut mango into bite-size pieces. Tear up
just a few of the mint leaves. Reserve some of
the fruit and whole mint leaves for garnish.

Place the rice in a large bowl and gently
fold in the fruit and mint. Then place the rice
and fruit into four individual bowls, evenly

divided. On the top of the rice and fruit mixture, make three or four flowers out of strawberry quarters, halved blueberries, and pieces of mango. Make centers for the flowers out of fruits of different colors. Tuck mint leaves in beside the flowers.

SERVES 4

# OSHI-ZUSHI

Pressed sushi is the oldest form of sushi, having evolved from the ancient practice of packing fish and rice together to pickle the fish. Today, rice and other ingredients, raw or cooked fish, and/or vegetables are pressed together in a mold to form a block. When the top is taken off and the mold is removed, the blocks are cut into bite-sized pieces. Traditionally, molds were made of wood; now there are handy plastic molds which are easier to keep clean and fresh. Any container with straight sides can be used as a mold by lining it with plastic wrap. A top to press down the rice can be made out of firm cardboard covered with plastic wrap. This kind of sushi can be made and kept at room temperature for up to six hours, depending on the topping. For this reason, it is a great type of sushi to serve to guests or for a party.

*The following quantities are for a 5-inch x 7-inch x 2-inch mold:*

*Sashimi and/or vegetables to equal about 1 cup*
*1/2 quantity (2 cups) sushi rice*
*1 teaspoon wasabi*

Place sashimi and vegetable ingredients in a flat pattern covering entire bottom of the mold. (If using a plastic or improvised mold, line the mold with plastic wrap so that the block of sushi will be easier to unmold.) Dab the filling with some wasabi. Wet your hands in vinegared water. Cover the filling with a layer of rice. If desired, add another level of sashimi and vegetables, and then of rice. Press down top of mold to compact the rice and other ingredient(s). Remove the top. If using a wooden mold, remove the sides and turn the block over. It is then ready to be cut into pieces. If using an improvised mold, once you remove the top, carefully turn the mold over and gently remove the block with the help of the plastic wrap. If not serving the sushi immediately, cover it in plastic wrap, and keep at cool room temperature until ready to serve.

As ingredients, you might choose cucumber and smoked salmon, cut into narrow strips of equal width, laid down alternately on the bottom of the mold. Small sprigs of dill make a nice garnish once the sushi is unmolded and cut. Another easy and tasty choice is halved shrimp laid down tightly side by side and garnished, once unmolded, with thin slices of lemon. Use whatever pleases your taste buds.

MAKES 16 PIECES

# TEMAKI-ZUSHI

Easy to make and delicious, hand-rolled sushi is the perfect party food. It can have just about any type or combination of fillings. Provide sheets of *nori*, a big bowl of rice and all kinds of ingredients for your guests to choose from. After a little instruction from you—go ahead, show off a little—they can have a great time making their own sushi. It should be eaten right away. *Temaki-zushi* is sometimes referred to as the Japanese taco!

*3 nori sheets cut in half*
*1/2 quantity (2 cups) sushi rice*
*Choice of fillings*

Cut the *nori* sheets in half. Place a piece of *nori*, shiny side down, diagonally across your

left palm toward your
thumb. Your hand
should be open. Wet
your other hand in vine-
gared water, and with it

place a golf-ball-sized piece of
rice on the upper part of the
*nori*. With your fingertips,
gently pat and spread the rice
down toward your palm.
Don't get any rice on the cor-
ners of the *nori*. Spread a thin line of wasabi
down the center of the rice. Place the fillings
lengthwise, along the wasabi line. (It's OK to
have some tips of the filling extend beyond
the upper edge of rice.) Dry your hands, then
fold the left corner of *nori* over the rice (it will
stick). Continue rolling upward to the right
until you end up with a cone-shaped *temaki-
zushi* ready to be eaten.

 Choose your favorite ingredients, in
whatever combination you
like, when making this kind of
sushi. One of my favorites
includes smoked salmon, scallions, avocado with wasabi,
and a squeeze or two of lemon

juice. For serving to friends, you can lay out all the ingredients, including a wide variety of fish and vegetables, and let them make their own.

MAKES 6 ROLLS

# INARI-ZUSHI

*Inari-zushi* is made from deep-fried tofu, called *abura-age*, cut in half to form pouches and then filled with sushi rice. It is another good party food, because, unless you use raw fish as an ingredient, it can be kept for many hours at room temperature. *Abura-age* is sold in markets and is easy to use; just be very gentle when you handle it. Simmered in a mixture of sugar, water, sake, and soy sauce, it makes a very tasty sushi stuffed with plain sushi rice. And it's even better when you add other ingredients.

*3 deep-fried tofu* (abura-age)
*3/4 cup chicken stock or* kombu dashi
*2 tablespoons sugar*
*1 tablespoon mirin*
*1 tablespoon shoyu*
*2 teaspoons sake*
*1/2 quantity (2 cups) sushi rice*

*Other filling ingredients of your choice (see the following recipe for Mushroom and Scallion Filling for* Inari-zushi)

● NOTE: *Kombu dashi* is made by simply soaking *kombu* in water for a couple of hours, heating on low to boiling point, and removing the *kombu*.

Place the fried tofu on a cutting board and roll each piece with a rolling pin. Place tofu in a bowl and pour boiling water over them. Let stand for one minute, remove, and drain. (This process removes some of the oiliness in the *abura-age*.) Then cut the pieces in half either lengthwise or diagonally. Gently open each piece at the cut edge to form a pouch. In a saucepan, bring chicken stock (or *dashi*) and sugar to a boil. Add the tofu and cook for three minutes at medium heat. Add the mirin, *shoyu*, and sake. Simmer for five minutes. (The liquid will reduce, so keep an eye on it.) Remove pan from heat, take out the tofu, and drain.

When filling is ready, squeeze excess moisture from the tofu and carefully open the pouch. Wet your hands in vinegared water, then take a golf-ball-sized piece of rice (plain or with other ingredients mixed in) and loosely fill the pocket. If your piece of tofu is square, you can turn the edge of the top back so the pouch looks like a bag, with the fillings visible. If you have a triangular-shaped piece of tofu, once filled it will look like a three-cornered hat. Or with either shape you can just fold over the top and seal with rice.

MAKES 6 POUCHES

# MUSHROOM AND SCALLION FILLING FOR INARI-ZUSHI

This is an especially tasty filling for the tofu pouches. You will think of all kinds of delicious combinations of ingredients using your favorite foods.

*2 dried shiitake mushrooms*
*3/4 cup water*
*1 tablespoon sugar*
*1 tablespoon mirin*
*2 teaspoons soy sauce*
*1 tablespoon sake*
*3 finely chopped scallions, white part only*
*1/2 quantity (2 cups) sushi rice*

Soak dried mushrooms in warm water for 30 minutes. Drain and reserve liquid. Cut the caps off and finely chop. Put 1/4 cup of the reserved liquid in a

saucepan with sugar, mirin, soy sauce, and sake, and bring to a boil. Add chopped mushroom caps and scallions, and simmer for 3 minutes over medium heat. Remove from heat and let cool. Once cooled, fold the mushroom mixture into the rice. Wet your hands in vinegared water, then divide the rice mixture into six portions and stuff into the tofu pouches.

MAKES 6 FILLINGS

# GUNKAN-MAKI-ZUSHI

Battleship sushi is one of the easier kinds of sushi to make. The rice and the *nori* make a cup or boat shape in which to put raw toppings that would not stay on top of *nigiri-zushi*. Traditionally, the toppings were various kinds of fish roe or small pieces of slippery raw fish. Inventive chefs now use many kinds of raw and cooked fish prepared in various ways, as well as some vegetable fillings. This type of sushi should be eaten as soon as possible after it is made, because the rice and moist fillings will cause the *nori* to get soggy and fall apart. If you are making several kinds of sushi, make *gunkan-maki* last.

*1/2 quantity (2 cups) sushi rice*
Nori *cut into strips 1-inch x 6-inches*
*Topping of choice*

Wet your hands in vinegared water. Roll two tablespoons of rice into a 2-inch x 1-1/4-inch oblong, about 1/2-inch thick. Press down gently. Place the rice shape on a moist cutting board. Dry your hands, then wrap the *nori* strip around the rice so that it overlaps. Use a smushed grain of rice to secure the seal. Place a small dab of wasabi in the center of the "boat" and fill with desired topping.

Toppings for this kind of sushi can be any kind of fish roe, chopped scallops sprinkled with lemon juice, guacamole, minced crabmeat, or whatever suits your fancy.

MAKES 12 PIECES

# NIGIRI-ZUSHI

Nigiri means, "to squeeze" in Japanese, and that is what an *itamae-san* does to the rice when he is making *nigiri-zushi* perfectly formed in size and shape. The rice should fall apart on your tongue, not all over the counter. The making of these sashimi-topped rice fingers looks simple when you are watching the chef swiftly creating them at the sushi bar. It isn't! Getting things to "hang together" just doesn't seem to happen easily for the beginning sushi chef. *Nigiri-zushi* is considered to be one of the most difficult sushi to prepare. With that in mind, the instructions given here are somewhat simplified and are (almost) guaranteed to prove successful. However, it's a good idea to review the "Important Tips for Sushi Success" (see pages 108-109) before you begin.

*8 ounces sashimi*
*1/2 quantity (2 cups) sushi rice*
*Wasabi*

Slice sashimi into 3-inch x 1-inch x 1/2-inch pieces, and arrange them singly on the damp cutting board. Wet your hands in vinegared water. Take a small handful of rice and gently roll it into a 2-1/2-inch x 1-inch oblong shape. Press your thumb into the top center of the oblong, making a dent. Turn the rice over and put a small dab of wasabi on it. (If you need to tidy up the shape of the rice, do so very gently.) Try to coax the rice into just a little bit of an arc shape. Place rice shapes on the dampened cutting board. Make as many of these shapes as you wish, lining them up on the cutting board. (Don't allow them to touch each other or they will stick together. If your hands are getting sticky, rinse them again in the vinegar water.)

Place pre-cut pieces of sashimi on top of rice shapes so they extend slightly over either end of the rice, and press down gently. With your thumb and third finger, carefully press the end of the sashimi into the rice at the same time you are gently pressing the sides with the fingers of your other hand. Your *nigiri-sushi* is now ready to serve.

MAKES 12 PIECES

Toppings for this sushi can be any kind of sushi grade fish that is available to you, if it is absolutely fresh and has been handled properly.

# MAKI-ZUSHI

Making rolled sushi is another challenge. The recipe here is for *hoso-maki,* or small *maki-zushi.* Once you have mastered this skill, you can move on to making the larger sizes, which have more rice, multiple fillings, and a full-size sheet of *nori.* Getting the hang of keeping the rice and filling where they belong, in the roll, and preventing the roll from splitting, takes some practice. Accidents usually happen because the roll is overstuffed, but this is less likely to happen with the smaller rolls. *Hoso-maki*, a very popular sushi at a sushi bar, is the easiest sushi to eat in one bite.

*2 sheets of* nori*, cut in half*
*1/2 quantity (2 cups) sushi rice*
*8 ounces assorted fillings*
*Wasabi*

Place the bamboo rolling mat down in front of you on your work surface, with the slats parallel to the edge of the table. Place *nori* on

the mat, shiny side down, with a wide side closest to you. Wet your hands in vinegared water. Place 1/2 cup sushi rice on the *nori* and gently spread it all over the *nori*, leaving a

one-half-inch border of *nori* on the far edge. Take a dab of wasabi and drag it across the center of the rice, making a thin line. Place the filling(s) on top of the wasabi in a continuous line. Dry your hands.

Raise up the end of the mat closest to you. With your thumbs underneath

the mat and your fingers holding the filling and rice in place, slowly and in a continuous motion roll the mat until you reach the end of the rice and the margin of *nori* is still exposed. Remember as you are rolling the sushi roll along that you don't want to roll it up in the mat. Tighten the roll by gently pulling back on the enclosed roll with one hand, and at the same time giving the far end of the mat a few gentle tugs; left, right, and center. Now, as before, roll a little farther and press gently so the two surfaces of *nori* touch each other and seal. Tidy up the ends if necessary and roll the mat back off the roll. Let the sushi roll sit for a bit, and seal down to make the seam more secure.

Lift the roll onto the cutting board. With your

very sharp knife, which you have wiped with a damp cloth, cut the roll in half. Then place the two halves side-by-side and cut them into thirds, yielding six pieces per roll. Repeat the whole procedure three more times.

Use any ingredients you choose for this sushi. However, you should use only one or two fillings, cut into thin slices. The classics are *tekka* (tuna) and *kappa* (cucumber).

MAKES 4 ROLLS, 24 PIECES

# URA-MAKI-ZUSHI

The inside-out roll is similar to *maki-zushi,* the difference being that the fillings and *nori* are on the inside and the rice is on

the outside. It is impressive, but takes some practice to get it just right. Usually the rice is coated with colorful fish roe or tasty toasted sesame seeds, black or white or both. The instructions for making this roll are very similar to those for *maki-sushi*, with regard to the rolling process, and you may find it no trickier to construct.

*2 sheets of* nori, *cut in half*
*1/2 quantity (2 cups) sushi rice*
*Toasted sesame seeds or fish roe (optional)*
*8 ounces assorted fillings*
*Wasabi*

Wrap the bamboo rolling mat in plastic wrap and place it in front of you on the work surface with the slats parallel to the counter. On a dry cutting board, place a sheet of *nori*, shiny side down, with the wide end closest to you. Wet your hands in vinegared water. Roll up 1/2 cup of rice into an oblong shape and place it the center of the *nori*. Spread the rice all over the *nori* with the tips of your fingers. Gently press the rice in place. If you like, sprinkle toasted sesame seeds or brightly colored fish roe all over the rice for extra texture and taste. Turn the rice-covered *nori* over and place it on the bamboo mat, wide side nearest to you. Draw a line of wasabi across the center of the *nori* and then place the filling(s) in a continuous line on top of the wasabi.

With your thumbs underneath the mat and your other fingers keeping the rice and *nori* in place, roll the mat slowly and steadily. Stop when the edge of the mat is straight down on the edge of the *nori* and enclosing the filling completely. Holding the roll in place, pull the mat gently toward you, and at the same time tug the far end of the mat, at the center and on both ends. Lift the front edge of the mat and continue rolling to seal the roll.

Unroll the mat and place the roll on a damp, smooth surface. If the roll is a bit out of shape, put the mat over it and gently squeeze into shape. Cut the roll in half, first placing a piece of plastic wrap over it if you like. Lay the two halves side by side and then, at the same time, cut them into thirds. Repeat the whole procedure three more times.

I suggest using shrimp, cut into thin strips, accompanied by thin strips of scallion, or tuna and avocado. See what kinds of interesting combinations you can come up with.

MAKES 4 ROLLS, 24 PIECES

# TEMARI-ZUSHI

This is a simple recipe for bite-sized sushi rice balls. They are ideal for serving at a party as canapés or as snacks for children. They take only minutes to make.

*Topping (smoked trout or salmon, tiny shrimp,*
  *thin slices of vegetables, etc.)*
*1/2 quantity (2 cups) sushi rice*
*Garnish*

Place a five-inch-square piece of plastic wrap on your work surface. Put a piece of topping in the middle of the square. Wet your hands in vinegared water. Shape a tablespoon of rice into a ball and place it on top of the topping. Pick up all four corners of the plastic wrap, and gather them together in the middle, close to the rice. Twist the plastic wrap to compact the rice and form a ball. Unwrap the rice ball. Place on a smooth clean surface, rice side down. Add a bit of garnish for the finishing touch on your *temari-zushi*.

NOTE: You could also make the rice balls without the topping and keep them in plastic wrap, at cool room temperature. Just before serving, unwrap the rice and add the topping.

MAKES ABOUT 24 RICE BALLS

# KODOMO-ZUSHI

Sushi for children of all ages is fun to make and pretty to look at. Using various shaped cookie cutters to mold the rice, and adding colorful toppings, you can create stars, flowers, and all sorts of other shapes for a fun snack food. You can make interesting canapés using very small cookie cutters. Note that open cookie cutters are preferable, as they facilitate pushing the sushi out of the molds.

*1/2 quantity (2 cups) sushi rice*
*1/2-3/4 cup toppings suitable for young children (Some suggestions include: thin omelet, smoked salmon, sliced or chopped cucumber, lightly cooked or raw whole or chopped vegetables, tuna fish salad, cheese slices, or cold cuts.)*
*Colorful garnish*

Wet the cookie cutters, and your hands, in vinegared water. Gently pack each cookie cutter with sushi rice. Press to firm up the rice. Gently lift the cookie cutter. Put topping on the rice and garnish.

MAKES 18-20 PIECES

# EDAMAME BEANS

*5 cups water*
*1 teaspoon salt*
*1 pound package of edamame beans*
  *in the shell*
*Sea salt*

Bring water and salt to a boil over high heat. Add the beans and bring the water back to a boil. Boil for about 1-1/2 minutes, no longer. Drain and toss with sea salt. May be served warm or cold.

# MISO SOUP

First make the *dashi*, or soup stock, then the soup itself, as described.

ICHIBAN DASHI (soup stock)
*4 cups water*
*3-inch x 5-inch piece of* kombu *(kelp)*
*1 handful of* katsuobushi *(bonito fish flakes)*

Place water and *kombu* in a saucepan and heat on medium flame. Remove the *kombu* as the water just begins to boil. Add the bonito flakes. Don't stir. As soon as the water comes back to a boil, remove the pan from the heat. When the flakes settle on the bottom of the pan, strain the mixture through cheesecloth

THE SOUP
*1 quantity of* dashi
*3-1/2 tablespoons medium grade miso paste*
*2 scallions, chopped*
*1/2 cup thinly sliced* wakame *(dried seaweed)*
*1/2 cup tofu, cut into 1/2-inch cubes*

Bring *dashi* to a boil over medium heat. Put the miso paste into a strainer and hold it over the boiling *dashi*. With a wooden spoon, rub the miso into the boiling stock. Stir the soup. Check for taste; if it needs more seasoning, add a little more miso. Remove from heat. Put the vegetables and tofu into four bowls, add the soup, and serve.

MAKES 4 SERVINGS

# SALAD

Use baby spinach, arugula, watercress, cucumber, and scallions—that is, green things. The addition of *wakame* and pieces of *nori* make interesting Japanese additions to a green salad. Use one of the following dressings.

# SOY DRESSING

*1/2 cup rice wine vinegar*
*2 tablespoons sugar*
*1 teaspoon soy sauce*

Whisk the ingredients together until the sugar is dissolved.

MAKES 1/2 CUP

# WASABI DRESSING

*1/2 cup rice wine vinegar*
*2 tablespoons olive oil*
*1 teaspoon wasabi paste*
*1 teaspoon soy sauce*
*1/2 teaspoon sugar*

Whisk together, then refrigerate and allow the flavors to meld for a day or so.

MAKES 1/2 CUP

party time!

When you feel ready to share your new-found sushi skills and knowledge, it's time to have a party and celebrate. Whatever kind of social event you choose to have, remember the Japanese principles of balance, beauty, and a warm and welcoming atmosphere. Here are a couple of suggestions.

With regard to dinnerware and serving pieces, you may not have all the traditional types that a sushi bar uses. It would be fun to have them and you may decide to make a few purchases, but you can also improvise. Use your imagination and you're sure to come up with good substitutes. Plates for serving sushi should be flat. Any small saucer can be used for soy sauce, and each guest should have his or her own.

Buy some paper-wrapped chopsticks. Your guests may not know how to use them, but you can show them how.

# A SMALL DINNER PARTY FOR 4 TO 6 GUESTS

## MENU

- *Miso soup with tofu, scallions, and* wakame

- *Small plate of tuna and flounder sashimi, garnished with watercress leaves and wasabi*

- *Smoked salmon and cucumber* oshi-zushi

- Inari-zushi *with mushroom and scallion filling*

- Temari-zushi *with tiny shrimp topping*

- *Sliced fruit—pineapple, orange, and banana slices*

- *Beverages—sake, beer, tea,* umeshu

For this small dinner party it would be nice to have some Japanese music in the background. Candles and a single flower or two add a touch of beauty to the table.

# A ROLLICKING PARTY FOR LOTS OF FRIENDS

## MENU

- *Edamame beans*

- *Green salad with wasabi dressing*

- *Make-your-own* temaki-zushi: *plates of nori, assorted fish and shellfish, vegetables, and a large bowl of sushi rice, all ready to be rolled up into cones. Instructions courtesy of the host(ess).*

- *Beverages—sake, tea, beer*

With this kind of party you could have a lot of fun decorating with Japanese lanterns, Japanese fish kites, small paper parasols, and other cheerful touches. Big bright

African daisies look wonderful on the table. The music should be modern; consider even getting a CD of karaoke music, which is very popular in Japan. This party is a non-traditional, have-a-great-time kind of celebration. Use your imagination!

Whatever kind of party you have,
just relax and enjoy!
I wish I could join you.

*Sayonara!*